Bastardi Puri

BASTARDI PURI

WALID BITAR

The Porcupine's Quill

Library and Archives Canada Cataloguing in Publication

Bitar, Walid, 1961–
    Bastardi puri/Walid Bitar.

Poems.
ISBN 0-88984-267-1

    I. Title.

PS8553.187755B38 2005   C811'.54   C2005-900142-9

Published by The Porcupine's Quill (www.sentex.net/˜pql)
68 Main Street, Erin, Ontario NOB 1TO

Readied for the press by Eric Ormsby; copy edited by Doris Cowan.
Typeset in Trump Mediaeval, printed on Zephyr Antique laid,
and bound at the Porcupine's Quill Inc.

Represented in Canada by the Literary Press Group.
Trade orders are available from the University of Toronto Press.

We acknowledge the support of the Ontario Arts Council,
and the Canada Council for the Arts for our publishing program.
The financial support of the Government of Canada through
the Book Publishing Industry Development Program is also gratefully
acknowledged. Thanks, also, to the Government of Ontario through the
Ontario Media Development Corporation's Ontario Book Initiative.

 Canada Council   Conseil des Arts
for the Arts   du Canada

 Canada

 ONTARIO ARTS COUNCIL
CONSEIL DES ARTS DE L'ONTARIO

Table of Contents

THEATRE

There are bodies into which a river flows,
but these aren't necessarily seas.
We're outraged by liquid duplicity
we barbarize with midsection blows
splashes make fun of with elusive ease;
what we thought pure is farrago.
So when I walk along the banks of the Nile,
I withdraw into noncommittal smiles.

And I'll non-concur if you take up
the cause of H2O's freedom to act.
I don't mind drama's cute licensed pups;
these have a crowd-pleasing right to attack
the Actaeons of the universe who peep
at box-office smash Diana's physique.
But rain and its minions are less of a draw,
with too little tragedy, too high a fall.

Still, water is sacred; without it life
would be as unthinkable as criss-crossing
oneself without a rib cage. Any paradise
insists that its faithful be made of something
that would find fire anomalous; ice
qualifies, last of the red hot Vikings.
It and other casualties may be canonized;
to whip is human, to be whipped divine.

9

THESEUS

It was I who plotted constellations.
That's how I libelled the starry night.
Sections of sky I kidnapped for ransoms of meaning
an astrologer paid me in instalments.
But when it came time to release the hostages,
no one arrived to claim them and they
became distances running out on us.

I found myself in line shoving for rationed miles —
most ancient kind of labyrinth, the line.
No Minotaur waited at its endlessness.
No turns measured freedom in its air.

I grew impatient, but had to be diplomatic
with certain refugees, Rhodesian ridgebacks
angry because their country's constitution had changed,
leaving them strays on the Earth.

The language we used didn't apply
to what preceded or would follow this life.
The words were local, like Swiss Francs,
and maybe eternal equivalents of Italians
and Yugoslavs hid assets in these phrases.
Could our dialect have been nothing more
than lucre of the dead sheltering from supernatural taxes?

I attended daily to corpses of animals.
Sardines of Lisbon starred on my funeral pyres.
You would have taken them for Didos, the attention I gave them.

I gave everything attention; my delirium came
with its own flying buttresses. Many courtiers
told me it was divine, though unlike other deities,
no matter how I tried, it couldn't be sacrificed or prayed to.

THE POSSE

We were all angry; some of us ranted.
Others stormed an armoury, and purloined a musket.
The wise man in the group chuckled with his knuckles.
His placid expression didn't betray a punch line
that fled to the hills after our coup failed
to replace generals with pomegranate — such aspirations!
Though all we lived in was prefabricated.

Now we're visited by autumn, and its advice,
that we hibernate, that we try to colour,
but we're not maples, not black bears,
stay warm in casinos without placing bets,
dealt cards endlessly like ticks of time
we groom one another's pompadours by picking out.

To keep such schedules this late in history is a joke
we play on ourselves, but we have a double life
as a posse hunting down the hallucinated *flâneur*
each of us would prefer to be — alas,

we're a mob, athletic and sweaty sans-culottes
fired up to win at any cost even if it means
being put in kilns by hippies, and coming out ceramic,
model rebels and model sheep. To flock is the thing ...
We're terrified of being left alone — this, by a unanimous vote.

SPORTS

My brand of surveillance, no need for gadgets —
spoils are divided between eyes and ears.
It's true I miss the latest in lasers.
But I have no trouble making out hatchets.

I work in privacy, and for that reason
they stuck a camera up my neighbour's asshole.
All day he's bent over mooning my soul.
'Beyond one's means,' they call his visions.

The tribes I'm dealing with don't prize language.
They sip away at it like grape juice.
The boys don't give it time to age.
No taste buds ... they even gnaw roots.

As for the main course, that's human flesh.
Where are the gods, the sacrifice theories?
No home base — the East is the West.
One day it's slaughter, the next touchy-feely

speeches about peace, bread and land.
What the words mean isn't part of the package,
like seven nights advertised in Baghdad.
The days are spent back home on the ranch.

One day I gave this bandwagon the finger
(unconsciously) — now I'm on some list.
They mispronounce me. I've become 'bitter'.
Some of the hangers-on even lisp,

which doesn't make them any less vicious.
Quite the contrary: they have more to prove,
insist I pose as tequila (I'm cactus).
Gentlemen, if you feel pricks in your stool,

they're not mine. They're from citizens
you recently paged to rat on the guests.
Every envious doormat a witness ...
Can hyperactive ones become hit men?

What for an encore in the next world?
No time and space there, lucre or turds —
just memory ... and what to do with it?
Eternity, after all, has some standards.

THE GILDED AGE

I was a gaucho who roamed the prairies
without turning them into appropriate pampas.
My mood was the fossil it would have been impossible
to leave of itself; these words are substitutes,
an anthem for a state whose independence
I declare to get it out of me for a moment.

I like to crash if not parties, portions of mind —
a boudoir, a solarium — in which each breath
is a karaoke cover of the picayune heart's subtler beat,
that Machiavel who manipulates a body as it sleeps,

and whispers, 'Wake up! Your eyesight buttresses
cypress or sky with ironic wavelengths
that realize what's seen is not the thing itself,
but a sprawling compromise, a ceasefire between
the space-time clique, and everything outside it.'

THE MECHANICS OF BANALITY

Can we brainwash that meditating yogi?
We must find part of him that's a car
whose brakes we'll sabotage under the stars.
Get mechanics to train one of our lackeys.

A man seated like lotus is irritating.
I don't know why; it's none of my business.
I have narrow views on physical fitness,
but I close my eyes when I spot a psyche.

It may be that I love to talk,
but when others do, I grate my own nerves
in a pre-emptive strike. I won't be scratched
by people or primates in some cozy pack,

though in the wild it's supposedly grooming —
I'm mixing up human voices with ape fingers —
I couldn't care less. I'm not into singing,
or anything else except making you suffer,

whoever you are; we haven't met.
We may some day; I'm in charge of security.
There are folks who get off watching the sun set,
and others who watch them for opportunities.

ILLEGAL RESIDENT

Those who've died, or who've never been born,
have no infantry, and aren't allied.
Yet they're somehow thrown together,
invisible dice with no chance for numbers.
A gambler sniffs them like a cheetah with a cold,
and abandons them to romantic infinity.

Candlelight sketches us huddled together.
Our underground patois must have been born
to keep wax and flame out in the cold.
We higher forms of matter are allied
with time, that shadow cast by infinity —
not my first choice, hanging out with numbers.

We pick up where we were let off, cold
as trumped-up charges that bring witnesses together
to remind us how far we are from infinity,
and how tricky it is to have already been born.
I wouldn't add to, subtract from, our number.
Mathematically, our fates must be allied.

Is it a Greek imperialist, our infinity
unaware we're not Troy, but actually cold
Africans from the Old World, a number
recklessly migrating north together
to evolve into Neanderthals more aligned
with the avalanches of the Alps? We're bored.

Although we multiply, we're stranded as numbers
without nativities, more created than born.
And so we worship gods with whom we're allied
and run our state-of-the-art hot and cold
blood to bathe divine bribes, infinities,
less rank if body and soul scrub together.

I can't quite believe myself; if I lie,
it's because words can't police like a number.
They're nostalgic for meanings where they were born,
many difficult to revisit — take infinity …
I promised them we would go back there together,
but frankly, travelling in groups leaves me cold.

I prefer the vertigo of being unaligned.
Let time mobilize for its phony war with infinity.
I'll watch, not that the space granted me has its act together.

FASTING

I took my time, then launched into the fray,
and when I look back at the patience I squandered,
I realize my nature is to wander.
The rush out to lunch was a betrayal,

a personality's attempt to escape
from the prison it not only deserves,
but labours in as a warden to serve
a desperate need to gaze and be gazed

at, feel powerful, powerless, split
right down the middle, an all too precise
line that we know doesn't clearly exist
like end of water, beginning of ice.

THE ISLAND PORCILE

The trick is to sleep without telling the eyes
which are mindless, and so easily fooled.
The objective world is programmed to prey
on narcissists willing to stare into its pools,

and what it discovers are false witnesses.
It doesn't let on; we don't care to know.
This unsigned contract is our instinct for business;
each wave conforms, except for the foam.

Those of us stationed here have been travelling.
The island addresses are largely squandered.
If they'd been money, we'd be gambling.
Every morning, we have nothing to launder.

One day we might ask: are we eternal?
We seem so makeshift, checking our watches,
these china shops we wear though we're bulls,
or hope we are. Maybe we're leeches —

how unbecoming that would be!
To think each of us, a self-styled explorer,
is high on the blood of a real odyssey's
heroine, sucking away at her pores,

and hallucinating like that Chinese general
who ran out of weapons, sent out a ship
to be rained on by the enemy's arrows,
replenishing his arsenal for the next trip.

Could this have happened, or was it a dream
of a drunken sailor whose idea of menace
was to invent things better than feats?
When he's a pigsty, a man hops his fence.

THE FOURTH PERSON

I've been narrating our life in the fourth person,
a thug who slit the other three's throats,
obsessed with liquidating their points of view,
and promoting nobody's in particular.

It was right to turn our selves into equal signs,
and chase the two sides of equations away.
We contradicted numerical laws to test
air raid sirens in an age before planes.

I hope when what we say steps out of our mouths
for a smoke, it denies it was ever inside,
pretends not to recognize us, then gives itself
and the frescoes on our palates away. After all,

you never know when you'll need to peel
the statuesque off your skin, and stripped as Galatea
slash the Pygmalion who says life is beautiful,
teach him the homely truth of murder — if it lies,

he can wake his wounds, and serve them up
a breakfast of alabaster quince, and on the side:
scalloped doubting Thomas that I am.

A NIGHT IN THE CAPITAL

My DNA was mapped: turned out much of it
made no contribution to whoever I was,
had members who drifted between constellations
determining my skin colour, propensity to cancer,
disclosed nothing about me or themselves,
these Bowery Boys of my chromosomes.

After years of wandering, I ran into some of them.
They didn't recognize me, but weren't hostile.
I'd surveyed so often, my eyes were well trained,
but here, at the terminus, was not much to look at.
I fell asleep, and only then, how exactly I forget,

did I find a way to buy my new friends a round.
We got plastered, and discovered we were all one,
until, the next morning, I had a change of heart:
better not to bet one's whole identity
on a single body. I preferred the idea
of being spread around — if meeting, then by chance.

CUSTOMS

You decide: will your autobiography
be performed out loud by a showman,
or be groomed by off-track bookies
suppressing the sentences, waiting for omens?

We bugged your home: the conversations
were rough notes. If you don't mind
we'll launder them. The ironed versions
won't be yours. They will be mine,

though in a footnote I'll acknowledge
many colleagues who stayed up late,
their sixth sense on the edge
of your bargain-basement seat

we'll soon reupholster. Do you think
that one or two intelligence agents
got the ball we're throwing rolling?
You noticed the state-of-the-art equipment

charity swivelled to channel your voices
daily onto the world-wide net?
A dungeon or light, expanding universe?
We become smaller and smaller in it,

and, as I say, it's all in the family —
your family that is. Mine never speaks,
is invisible, some would say heavenly
in an earthy way. I spilled their beans

because I believed language that month
was beans. It's possible to say anything,
and believe anything. Take the word 'assassin':
two asses, the soul's, the body's — no sin.

I rest my case and I have no case,
no baggage to open (that would be torture).
I can only possess the beings I chase —
laid-back and coquettish, like now, I'm bored.

GUERRILLA

I was born in a city that would soon be destroyed.
I immigrated to the centre of the world.
After the long trip, I fell asleep.
I dreamed that he who wakes up steals

whatever he remembers of the state he snaps
out of, although he isn't branches,
it isn't a tree, and there is no reason
to feel guilty about changing — let seasons

bring back or kill life. I'm indifferent.
Comparisons to hit men or good Samaritans
will not break my allegiance to snow
which accumulates, but never grows.

If only I too could fall this way,
cover the ground instead of get buried
in it and then — the end justifies the means —
melt into the population, disappear.

PROGRESS REPORT

We waited for news; we were old-fashioned,
and didn't realize our patience was futile.
We live in an age whose executions and trials
are kept well away from the three dimensions,

away from time even — justice is eternal.
And so, for some reason, are our criminals.
At least that's what we're told in the papers:
no more arrests, and no more judges.

Here's to stereotypical searches,
poking the mind with asinine fingers,
to equality's rectums (his and hers).
Who can tell the coppers from the nurses?

I couldn't care less about human judgment,
including my own. Any point of view,
the hired libeller's, or the lawsuit's,
is a foreigner with a laughable accent.

Still, there have been days I regret
when wars that were raging excluded my causes.
Rounds of ammunition punctuated my pauses.
I made my living correcting a grammar

I had no faith in. At Teacher's Lounge,
a bordello near campus, at Hotel Arhaba
(the sign lost its M), in flocks of truths and lies,
the black sheep behaved just like the whites.

Unlike a priest, when I adjusted my collar,
it had no meaning for this congregation
whose *Weltanschauung*, like nuclear fission's,
was so worldly it blew off all the others.

Many, too many, of these wasted perspectives
glide now over our scarecrow Bastille
without any instinct to set us free.
Revolution is air — they're insouciant birds,

and so, at most, can be recreated.
How do they help us, all our frescoes,
always earthbound, inevitably argot?
We'll never speak the language of a court.

PANOPTICON

I write clearly to exorcise clarity.
When I'm abstract, I know it's escapist.
I'm never silent enough when I'm brief,
and rambling on can't compete with existence.

Nevertheless, reality tantalizes.
You want to reach out, and make it your hands —
next thing you know you're holding some prize,
a kitsch statuette. It strikes up a band,

and that of course is very surprising,
as if one of the truth's immune systems
mistook you for the latest virus
(one gypsy can alarm a camera of fascists).

I've certainly noticed the powers that be,
farcical or sublime, see and aren't seen.

PASHA

One moment words are refugees from Troy,
the next Greeks desperate to reclaim Helen.
They have no loyalty — boy toys may stick
to their native tongues, but then comes heaven
where language, that Falstaff, can't follow its Hals.

No dictionary taught me how to rule my lands.
I threw the Hippocratic oath into evidence,
so the child would have to drown or swim,
and doctor wave after wave of testimony
to convince our jury the sea was insane.

This worked. Encouraged, I turned on mountains,
claimed they were a frozen music
the soaring temperatures left unexplained.
So I imposed an atonal rule,
martial hits mostly, because in the past
silence had ignored my romantic overtures.

Syllables that survived I divided and ruled
until not one sound had a reputation,
good or bad. Created equal,
they returned to the democratic womb.

I was no Ottoman; this brand of politics
stripped me of laws, courtiers and subjects.
On the other hand, spies sent from Vienna
were no more dangerous than pastry chefs.
There was nothing for them to discover;
they invented new flakes, new jams ...

I sampled these, and sometimes enjoyed them.
One day I may immigrate to the West;
that way I can take part in its conquest
of what I used to be, perhaps still am.
A worst-case scenario: I'll become self-possessed.

007

He makes pocket money reporting my words,
and I don't mind; he's a family man.
The kids need skateboards, and the wife pans.
He licks every crumb, leaves nothing for the birds.

I wonder whether he numbers his pages.
Maybe each index card is autonomous.
Tasmanians are extinct, but their platypus
survives, eloquent memoirist of the ages.

Some people simply must write about strangers.
Though their expertise lies in the first person,
they sacrifice it on the altar of arson —
tautologies begin: fire is fire.

Who am I to criticize such sincerity?
It's almost selfless to become obsessed
with another, the inflated rhetoric an abscess
in the researcher's skin, his capital city.

ABSTRACTION

We have forgotten the gene pool we came from,
but it remembers us very well,
grasps at our backs in unsuccessful leapfrog,
premonitions, some say, of hell.

But I think we should make a distinction
between occasional slips of the tongue,
and the sharp, glaring hooks of fiction
on which damned carcasses will be hung.

These practical jokes they play in heaven!
I am not sure if it beggars belief,
but the template would seem to be Samson
and what he did to the Philistines,

except that our powers that be are not blinded,
though many they kill they've never seen
because they're always looking behind,
checking for shadows, not history.

I, who am hired to paint their portraits,
fully realize this idea is bad.
I tried to back out at the last minute —
lucky for me, my art is abstract.

ANONYMOUS

The hours promenade without a pedigree.
Mongrels come with more respectable pasts.
Some call hours guests, enjoying a spacious
hospitality, but they're hosts,
and we who arrive can never be sure
we're being thoroughly entertained.

Needless to say, we legislate laws,
fake doldrums; the real ones are equatorial.
They're a dolce vita lacking Latin script,
a strong and silent illiteracy we plagiarize;
it doesn't make the ancient mistake of committing
madness or sanity to the page, an asylum
in which there's so much time to regroup.

Now order is at home in wastes of time,
like a camel perfectly adapted to deserts;
I have been nothing more than a Bedouin
riding my beast around, drinking its milk,
and when times were bad, slaughtering it for meat,
which may be wrong — if so, I don't mind.
I have been right, and that gave me no pleasure.

BAKSHEESH

The places we've never been to are only moods.
They're invisible, but refusing to accept this
we project slides onto an iron curtain,
and are amused at how corrupt these eidolons are,
like bodyguards we slip a little baksheesh to —

in a flash, there we are, face to face with their leader,
the product of centuries of inbreeding.
His Majesty drools, stares at the ceiling.
Port is being served, and can it be? Gazpacho.

It's announced I'm the ambassador from El Dorado.
My poverty is a cover; I've stashed the wealth.
'No,' I say, 'it isn't me.' I look around
at the seated dancing midgets, the poker-faced fool.
I realize they know it isn't me, and don't care.
They need new games. They've run out of themselves.

TIME STANDS STILL

One day I laugh my head off — it's fun.
The next morning I've been guillotined.
I concentrate on a camp of has-beens.
I'm all of them. I have to run

to catch up with these ancient identities.
Even the dead ones have afterlives
(unruly, they sometimes break out in hives).
My last request is to live in a city.

That too is repeated over and over.
I wouldn't know what to do in the sticks —
turn into cactus, and count the pricks?
In France, they had Revolution and Terror.

Here, nothing changes. I'm still swamped
by sea creatures destined to be chimps.
No aristocracy flashes its pomp,
and no working class struggles to be free.

LOCAL COLOUR

The black paella again — it's Monday.
We used to serve up fighting bull stew
drenched in adrenaline; that was unhealthy,
said doctors who studied out in the blue.

The globe loves its citizens, and vice versa,
though globes we can see are always reduced,
as if the real size, like a Pre-Adamite Bertha,
would elicit catcalls from our poltroons.

I see no other audience in the mist.
Romantic weather obscures all the faces.
I try to recreate whatever I miss,
and pencil in falls I guide from grace.

Dairymaids taught me this alpine malice,
so much so it needs pasteurization.
Either we resort to the extreme artifice
of morality, or we have to come clean,

and learn to step on one another's toes
in slapstick rehearsals for the dance of death.
With a little coaching, we can forgo
feet, partners, and steam solo as breaths.

A REAL CHARACTER

Would I care to play chess with the boys?
Can't answer now — there's a call from Rio.
I'm not free; a life-loving voice
breaks down a door I thought was open.

You can never be open for real
unless you're air; even that bastard
is part of a production: the atmosphere.
When his run ends, I think I'll cast him

in one of my plays; a leading man
should be invisible. One particular face
excludes all other also-rans.
Why not a hero who's the race,

all other races, extinct ones too,
animal, human and the missing links?
We have so many — never enough room
to take up what their character is.

CODED MESSAGE

Our senses of humour occupied the other five,
which put up only a token resistance
like yokels who don't know how to dance
surrendering to polkas in a smoky dive

they choose to feast on dumplings and beer.
Oh, don't you shudder at such grotesque dates
that fill rumbling bellies with carbohydrates?
There's really no choice. We must intervene

with peacekeepers even though there's no war.
The locals must be taught cantaloupes,
watercress sandwiches, and to say 'oops'
when they step on the toes of a whore,

an imported word, though no apology —
that's the idea: some condescension.
No, correct that: 'sophistication'.
Those who can't catch on we can kill.

PROTEUS

It was a golden age. Speaking of which,
where have the damsels in distress run off to?
We knights have nothing better left to do
than polish our arms and our fingernails
for a camp crucifixion of the slender Messiah
sent down to suffer in stuffy drawing rooms,
to accidentally knock over the hostess's Tanagra …

Nevertheless, there's hope rumours will surface.
They went out for a swim; some say they drowned.
But I'm sure they'll return to the villa refreshed.
We gossip about rumours when they disappear,
and so they return to change the subject,
to convince us they're each a form, not its content.
I've learned by their example: I too am a form,
and what I say says nothing about me. I remain

what some call pure, some call blank.
On occasion, my desire was to be unreal,
to have that privilege, be here and not here.
The choice between the two I treated like spring,
and turned it into summer whenever I pleased.
I never asked myself what summer was,
lay out in the sun, grew dramatically dark.
Looking back on it now, I must admit
I like what's become of my skin, and want it darker.

BLAGUE

Courteous Bertolt, why not strum
banjos for the deaf and blind?
Pure vibrations are more fun
if lyrics and music are left behind

with all the other excess baggage
we pikers will not dish out for.
Say what you please; we are sages
free to open those closed doors

that aren't locked. And if they are,
we can feel or fake indifference
after a few shots at the bar,
hand-delivered, though heaven-sent

as is the rent we pay the landlord
every month in pantomime.
We pretend we're Mongol hordes
in absent costumes which he buys.

THE BREAKING OF TOYS

Some days there are untold compositions,
then comes the odd lunation with none.
Maybe we write when we need more tombs;
is our silence, then, not having a prayer?

We only have words for what's dead inside us,
said one man; another, deceased,
had claimed culture meant burying corpses.
Poets and gravediggers are athletic priests,

but what, I wonder, lies under my lines?
What, exactly, is no longer living?
I probably don't need to know, and besides
if it's a B-movie, there might be zombies.

To make fun of our souls is vaguely modest,
but needless to say, it's also a ploy,
a traditional way to avoid arrest;
we play with our lives, then break the toys.

SURVIVAL OF THE FITTEST

Our ancestors wouldn't know what to make
of us if they were here; we're their immortality,
which they may enjoy at heavenly stages,
but back down in this bombed-out city

we're cannon and fodder for sight's artillery.
Light isn't reflected off objects into us.
We fire the world out of our sockets, real
only in so far as demigods we trust

say so. We wait for news and entertain
ourselves by sampling our favourite scams:
selling the auctioneer's tongue as it auctions,
clapping with our earrings instead of our hands …

We're not an audience for opening nights.
We interrupt actors because we're bored
and angry enough to rewrite their lines.
Our idea of socializing is to forge

one another's signatures at struggle meetings
modelled on Maoist peasant scenes,
except that now we pull enough strings.
The self-criticism of each human being

describes foreign bodies — a hippopotamus,
or the sun with its repetitive rising and falling
valuable as a gold mine immune to rushes,
or, in my case, the Loch Ness monster.

I'm restless at rest, though when in motion
longing for stasis. So I've found a compromise
and become a figment not of my imagination,
but of somebody else's. That's how one survives

after he's gone, and I'll be leaving soon.
The neighbours are trick-or-treating. I'm out
of the usual candy — give them ships of fools,
laws of hospitality on automatic pilot.

Here's my strategy: I'll welcome them into
my study, the drawers and the garbage pails
that are spilled, jumped on, occasionally hurled
across the floor we mop up for stage names

fit for a tomb. If we sleep at the wheels
of post-Darwinian worlds, our survival
means manic rehearsals and depressing revivals
of agnostic takes on the Lazarus theme.

THE CONSOLATION OF BLASPHEMY

Though I listen, I don't hear what you say.
I know that for others you are divine,
visit their sleep to answer their prayers,
but you and I don't have conversations.

I never got a word in, didn't try
before today. But now here I am
preferring, like most men, lines to deeds,
talking at someone I don't understand

in the abstract, haven't seen in the flesh,
talking because an insomniac's
body sooner or later genuflects
in exhaustion that resembles respect,

apparent worship of some higher force,
high as Caligula who had a favourite,
made him a senator though he was a horse.
What shall I make of my self-hatred?

THE CAMERAS OF VERONA

Why make appearances if they're merely of your self?
Turn the tyrannical mirror into a deferential tool,
a Polonius whose tedious imagery isn't followed,
except by cameras, and they can't even speak his language.

I'll re-educate them; what's this morning's
exchange rate for pictures into words?
Your mug will be lost in translation, martyred.
I'll charge no commission. I'll donate
the cause of my didactic zeal to a war

that has no cause; its shootouts make no sense,
and can't be explained even by your top soldier,
his ignorance and mine a Romeo and Juliet
we forbid to wed. And yet, as usual, they manage to elope.

GRAND TOUR

And so I became eternity's pied-à-terre;
it used me once or twice a year.
The rest of the time I went to seed.
Dirt streets I'd been gentleman of were paved.

As for the wilderness I tried to sleep in,
its gaga fertility now censored news,
and like evil eyes, those Crusader blues,
infested alphabets with prostrate ivy.

Oedipus made the headlines; any prophet
knows spoken words are patricidal boys —
sly, they swim up on their own vocal cords
like Pacific salmon, and not only to mate.

Their so-called souls are easy to buy,
these prodigies we hire to decorate fate.
But tough Muses follow; they too gravitate
to our centres of power — arrest them, they're spies!

BIO DIVERSITY

There were days you ran around,
and others you slept through, but I
cannot remember how I found
the trick to turn your space and time

into the ones that I live in.
I speak not as biographer.
You have been reincarnated —
your autobiography, my dear,

is what I'm working on from now
to an eternity, for death
won't break our lucrative concentration.
I became you in good health,

and will be you as we decompose
into our prose, which is immortal.

CTESIPHON

I hear the best passports are yet to come.
I see nations with the third, second, first person
rolled into one, each a citizen who loses track of himself,
even as he makes bigger and bigger impressions on whatever that self is,
maybe an enemy, maybe a friend, who doesn't come into focus,
a picture never prepared to be taken,
almost a fortress.

You want to besiege the thing, and catapult boulders in until
you remember it's you — you who once left
your front door unlocked, and now have to knock,
a guest at your own shoulders.

One approach might be correspondence:
pretend the front is the back
side of a postcard, so whatever you write looks like graffiti
on the Venuses de Milo, the Arcs of Ctesiphon,
the views of Land's End.

What's said is hypothetical. After all, you can't see,
no more than paint can, and you can't hear,
no more than sound. Your skull, as if biting
the mouth that fed it, pokes through your skin,
decomposing tropically; your ears seem
to make mincemeat of words.
The consolation: they'd make mincemeat of thought

escaping you into embassies of air,
asylums no one follows it into.
The present, that inaudible chord,
seems to be on strike, each of its atoms
an antic disposition put on by a god.

What duty could they be avoiding,
these infinite creatures, to evacuate themselves
from their demanding identities, and hide out in you?
They could be speaking now — if so,
they chose their positions so as not to be heard.

AN APPARATCHIK

As for the self-knowledge of an apparatchik,
it's openly bundled up and stored
some places convenient, in huts or attics.
Like a call waiting, it's put on hold,

which clears room for facts about strangers.
What am I saying? Creates a vacuum
into which rush, disguised as hot air,
statistics compiled by venal grooms

for whom dirt is as good as a dowry.
Who are the lucky ladies of dreams?
Oh, they're the ones the party is deflowering
while you and I are trying to sleep.

In the old days I was one of the gang.
Some nights, if they ask, I still lend a hand.

VACATION

A weekend of polite conversation,
bliss ... my opinions hang out with tongue —
they get all excited, these splashed myrmidons
when they see a bridge they haven't burned.

They sign for me *here* that I botched my life,
decided to christen my bluff its bluff,
so it could be the illusion and I
nab a second act as a poker-playing tough.

'No, I'm a masochist,' I say, 'a skinflint
who formulated his ideas to provoke
a free cat-o'-nine service — the trick
was unconscious at first. Then it became known' —

and that's not true either, my shimmy to line
the beautiful deluge with ugly reasons.
Next, I'll invite an abolitionist to dine
with a master. Now won't that be fun?

Dear gentlemen, you have more in common
than you'd care to roll in the grave.
You and I, our debates vacation —
all expenses are paid by the slaves.

AN EPIPHANY

An epiphany in a city of concrete blocks?
Dissect your brain; it isn't any prettier,
nor are its cadaver's other neighbourhood spots —
the inner world is less picturesque than the outer

when viewed in the three dimensions that moonlight
as the Fates, so busy with these occupations
they have no time for private lives
they wouldn't enjoy, being inhuman.

But I, I'm such a social lion
I'm determined to lure them out of their state.
The Garden of Eden had its serpent,
and space must somehow deal with my hate;

its surfaces naturally take to my spying.
They'd rather not do dirty work alone,
and are always ready to donate their disguises
to the right charity, one like oblivion.

THE DIPLOMATIC DISTRICT

The domesticated version is in an hourglass,
but how differently time behaves out in the wild.
If I were a mime, I'd whip it up into marble, and chisel away.
I'd invigorate the scene by staring idealistically
off into the distance, half Soviet sickle wielder, half
aesthete double-crossing sunsets with the eyes

reality rarely reaches. Most often it sends ambassadors,
some trained to be things, teapots, gourds,
others more extravagant, bougainvillea,
discarded underworlds of fly-by-night mythologies
to remember is brutal activity, a stringing up
of what would prefer to live on in original shadows
reproduced now, blowing their immortal lines and cover.

THE MARIACHI OF HEAVEN AND EARTH

The sting of conscience isn't what it used to be.
You wait for insects to do the work for you.
It's only natural your wars are skin-deep.
Masseuses are more useful than beliefs
in your space and time, plaster casts
in which perception insists on recovering
although it has never been accurately broken.

While your back is rubbed, you often remember
the similar fingers and care of espionage,
the intimate servility of attending to a man
you don't know and care desperately about,
as if he were your soul, and you some pilgrim.

Your mind won't be at ease till you sack our capital.
What joy you'll experience, and how quickly you'll get bored …
First we play indifferently, then we lose the play,
are left to ad lib and confuse the other actors

who still go by the book after a peripeteia.
Such chaos does wonders for our characters
we should interpret lazily; they're inexhaustible,
and can easily shake off any sweat we work up.

Our poppies are slaughtered, unaware they're opiates.
And we urbanites, perhaps we're also contraband.
I'm not the introspective type; I can't be sure
what effect I'd have ground into powder, smoked.

THE GOOD, THE BAD AND THE UGLY NEWS

If you dissent, we'd care to listen —
you know what I mean (for the next ten years).
Some have a Hector, some an Achilles;
we have bugs, and undercover sex kittens.

Make our selves clearer? That's not the rage.
We researchers used to be understood
before democracy. Now we're free to skate
where there's no ice. We can eat sans food.

Meanwhile, big boys run the restaurants,
kitchens, supermarkets, slaughterhouses,
hustling Cupid's wings and his bows,
bought by young suits (we arrows are writers).

Boys and girls, what subject shall we cover?
All depends on the protagonists' names.
We have strict orders; somebody called Arthur
wouldn't fit in, regardless of his crime.

A Jill would work, and so would a Jack —
these have a role to play in our game.
But if a coup is staged by a Mac,
we bury it somewhere in the back pages.

Our chic publishers refuse to explain
what each buzz word signifies to insiders.
They call the shots; we must be lame,
compose as ordered or be fired.

As for our morale, Montesquieu says freedom
is the freedom to follow the law.
The deal was the same when we were in kingdoms —
it's an old tradition, buying our souls

which, by the way, are so beautiful!
We're a community; let's all hold hands,
and meditate fixed on that window sill,
or Persian carpet. Ignore the glass.

The views you think are there are illusions,
at least this month. Maybe in March,
if MPs declare war on the sun,
we'll say it burned (stabbed) our backs,

the arrogant, overrated terrorist,
whose Christian name, by the way, is William —
we'll shorten it. Ignorance may be bliss,
but that's nothing compared to our owners' whims.

PORTER'S LODGE

You turned out to be waking dreams
I, like a fool, fell fast asleep for.
Come back, so you'll see and be seen
in the sunlight I used to abhor.

As usual, I've gone back on my word,
and left the cave I planted my flag in.
I can explain: the echoes were traitors,
stripping voice of internationality.

The atmosphere grew all too provincial,
as duelling banjos and campfire
subtracted each self from its shadows,
dancers shrugging shoulders with the Furies

who, passing through, bored in between jobs,
stepped on some toes, and then chopped them off.

SPAGHETTI MIDWESTERN

Is slander illegal here? Lord, no!
It's a sign of wealthy human nature.
Without rococo connections, we're subject to slurs
of those whose beliefs are their employers';

these can be easily learned by rote.
The average errand boy knits brow and bunkum;
desperate for tenure, his wild oats
are sown carefully on mothers and nuns

who, unlike cotton, take needle and thread
with a grain of salt. Don't lactate,
ladies, or your powers will go to the head
of our teetotalling scribbler, lover of fate

only if it comes with clear instructions
that give him green lights to be original,
claim to be the first to admire mule dung.
In my hometown, we prefer the animal,

and to our professional that too is swell
(the fewer the enemies, the smoother a career) —
he'd happily lick every ass in hell
if he could get a visa; he's law-abiding, our seer.

Alas, not every nation has an embassy.
The sublime ones don't even keep consuls.
There's only one way he can pass on the ferry —
anaesthetize him. Say you're taking out the tonsils.

DEVELOPING COUNTRIES

Though eyewitnesses insist history's sleep is light,
it's rather heavy, and hardly stirred
if a bottle breaks in an alley, used as the chronicler is
to winking with a hotelier's Brummagem composure.

The next thing you know lobster and iguana
are mistaken for viola and violin
in kitchens whose acoustics have in them a Spartacus
to lead the others in revolt, muffling any fugue.

I'd drown it out by landing helicopters,
metal teabags to the boiling gods,
as any make-up man knows, and my conscience,
which is a lagging indicator, an unemployment rate.

PRODIGAL SONS

We pause, reflect … this doesn't make us mirrors.
Worlds inside and outside man have little
to do with one another, like brothers
separated at birth. Both are prodigals.

One is homeless, and the other hops a ship
to cruise round the globe; they never meet.
Naturally, they're told they have relatives,
and thinking it over, one may believe.

The other has doubts. He thinks of the past
as shelter for people far above the fray.
He's a sailor, the flotsam and jetsam
are family enough, and then the obvious waves.

Pray for the dirty blond landlocked twin
whom nothing resembles: may he grow a shark's fin.

A CHAIN COLLISION

Your ex-owner thinks you're dead; he paid.
I asked him about his spendthrift hatred.
He said his first choice was an *auto-da-fé,*
but he had no books. He isn't inquisitive.

See, you and Alexandria's ancient library
cast similar spells on our backroom swine.
But look at yourself; you're dirty and hairy
and this music I play you isn't mine.

Set records straight? Settle the score?
We live in a bordello; why check for clean towels?
Consonants are gigolos, so are vowels.
Yet less is not necessarily more.

The truth about lingo: you can say anything.
Here's how it sets off to make its fortune:
it enters ear after ear without knocking,
intrepid miner, and rediscovers tin.

You may object that we are the speakers,
but we're useful middlemen, nothing more.
Where sentences come from is where they disappear.
Their bodies faint when we perfume their souls

with wild opinions we once held —
it seems to me they held us back
from a precipice they were,
and yet I miss them, bored with tact,

bored too with angels now descending
from the heavens to judge before
we turn lovable, eternally sleeping.
Let them land their crashing joy,

these insects who teach us practicality,
how to crawl, and how to sting?
I'm being unfair; I know they fly.
I won't begrudge them golden wings.

Ah, but the strain of exploiting their lingo …
Something informs me it's a proletariat,
and I'm the big bad capitalist hobo
scheming with silent partners, alley cats,

to take over the world that's in my head,
squatting there — could it be even poorer
than those of us mistaken for dead
every other night? My *Schadenfreude*

would like to say yes, but never does,
too busy with its 'Workers of the World, Unite',
which is another way of saying to the suckers
'You're as divided as night and day: good night.'

To make amends, I'll grant independence
to you, smelly beast and spiritual son.
It's not in our nature to be incense.
Stick to buying, selling and burning the stuff,

each in his hut. If you must, use temples.
But let the transport, when it comes, be free.
Bodies, after all, shouldn't have to travel,
and souls, being fictions, can make up currencies.

INSTEAD OF A RIDDLE

I know that arguments entertain,
but I have no proofs to support my needs
to see through glass when it is stained,
pretend it's a mirror when it is clear,

to listen closely for nothing being said,
then blank out at the full-blown thesis.
Can't make out disciples. What I have instead
is a big ego in too many pieces.

The millions of breaths that I have committed
are all, in my mind, a play in one act
that I should at least consider a riddle,
but I can't think of a question to ask.

THE WHITE MIDDLE SEA

You have armed your identity to wage a war
of attrition on the Californian hired to play it,
with no subtitles preserving your native tongue
that may be Balkanized by some angry young Turks
unless wrapped up in invincible tinsel.

Legumes have evolved less artificially.
That's what allows them to thrive in mud,
and maintain a dignified bearing, while we
would need an alibi, such as wrestling Amazons
who arrive each fortnight on Albanian ferries.
The Adriatic lacks the finesse of the Styx.

Tackiness hasn't drafted its patron saint.
Lost and desperate causes have Isabel la Católica —
now vinyl must be saved, merry-go-rounds,
strippers with pythons, even underage souls
not chaperoned by their torsos.

Our ports of call have partial bodies for dress codes,
and these ship in as masterpieces in oil,
refusing to surrender their coats to customs.
There's pride in Anonymous's self-portrait,
but canvas fights for its plain independence —
it harangues his paint, his glands, like cheap deodorant.
I miss our natural orator, the not too distant past.

TARZAN

In wrestling and poetry, everything is staged.
Contestants rehearse their pins and holds.
For artifice to work, it must be faked;
those with the least sincerity soar.

One can spin a tale of self-sacrifice
best if his temper finds heroes vain.
Feeling every word one utters is a swelling
that warps a surface, and bruises the fun.

Hard to be certain; it often happens
we can't decide if we mean what we say,
a state never listed with the deadly sins,
this taking of pleasure in our deep disarray.

Friends, it bores me to know where I stand;
a meditating Tarzan needs quicksand.

SHAHRAZAD

Do you mind if I call you Shahrazad
as we wait for our life to turn into a story
you postpone by not telling me?

We may be hallucinated, but we're not concerned,
having friends in high places, Himalayas, anthills,
and countless speed bumps of the soul.
I'll be discreet; I won't name moguls.

Instead, I'll confess my mind has weather,
an eternal spring we Cuernavacans reside in
that won't listen to reason; it believes tsunamis
are the ecstatic ghosts of kamikazes.

Sometimes the most rigorous way to hunt
is to realize, from the beginning, there's no quarry,
but a hyperactive taking of the air, sniffing dahlias,
a mystic, for example, might perform calmly.

My mind is so crowded — not by actual mobs —
by their debris. Bits and pieces of frenzy take up
much more room than one coherent outburst.

And my skin is a bodega for lice whose thirsts
would have made me rich if they'd paid the tab
I let them run up, because I thought at the time
it was the noble thing to do; my morality
had its waiters, waitresses, maître d',
whose existence it ignored as if to evade
wages by denying it ran a business. It did,

and made millions in silent conversations whose dialects
were the square roots of words, the creatures themselves.
See them in the Cacatua Galerita cage?
Just like them to prefer shade to high noon.
Language and I, we came from the same wilderness,
and now we've ended up in zoological gardens.

A RING

In a past life, I was a Black Russian.
Now I work as an informer on the spirit I was,
but cold eyes I try to cast on saloons
land on my own sobriety, reduced to telling tales.

Once upon a time, we all fell down.
We must have been singing ring-around-a-rosy
before the catastrophe, dancing in circles,
as medieval ladies and gents did to show
the plague who's who. It didn't get the message,
kept mixing everyone up, and probably
still wouldn't admit there are people one kills,
and others one doesn't — if one has eyes.

I always thought mine were stored in the attic,
yet I own no home, and rent no space.
Where could eyes be kept — in studios, like femmes fatales?
If so, not by me. My luck if some financier
in a flat with mirrored ceilings, and psychedelic lights
keeps them for his own dastardly pleasure.

Look: a massive midwife mispronounces over and over
my guttural birth. Perhaps I'm being born again,
so lazy I can't be bothered to ask her. And who's to say
she'd give an honest answer? Better to wait patiently.

Some grand event will come along and abduct me,
a fashion show — that's a dependable terrorist.
But the ransoms it receives are attention spans
too tall and slim for a classless revolution;
peace, bread and land become pants.

When it comes to wardrobes like mine,
every hour of the day is a bouncer; I won't be let in,
won't be kept waiting either, and have to hustle up
timeless ways to pass the afternoon. Luckily,
my ego doesn't mind having nothing
projected onto it; there are holes on its screen,
and a picture show doesn't work half as well as a blackout.

FALSE ORESTES AND THE NANOSECONDS

Who's behind me? Do Furies ride mopeds?
Maybe ... that certainly isn't my shadow.
I know I've been a very naughty biped.
Hope they send bona-fide nannies to whack me.

With my luck, I'll get some MPs
(zealous campaigners, not innocently drafted).
I know these types; they don't slap wrists.
They wolf down asparagus so that the pee

passed on miscreants is memorable.
Yet I, widely known to suffer from amnesia,
won't benefit from any search or seizure
of my preference for the ineffable.

A guy has the right to control emissions —
never from our vegetarian politicians.

FATA MORGANA

Since my recesses departed for Fata Morgana,
I've had to stalk my vision; it has many offers.
If I knew from where, I'd cut it off at the pass,
or at least pitch a tent, receive my wavelengths,
welcome them like strangers, slaughter something —
guests must be fed — and wait for their turning out to be angels

able, of course, to see through me, see
I'm an actor, a man who memorizes himself,
who takes his applauded Arlecchino home with him, and goes on
quarrelling with Columbina even as he bathes, sleeps, dreams …

A part of me says this is what immortality must be.
But my unconscious mind disagrees; it has exited
like a brawling scholar to some mountain temple,
to rivers and valleys I haven't heard of
that it's now painting, and when it's finished I'll sense.

Until then lack of curiosity is my only landscape,
though the bamboo, stone, waterfalls, birds
have been replaced by shadows of themselves.
I'm in no rush to locate the originals.
I know they'll come, as I know everything will. One day,

they'll all arrive together: the angels, the strangers,
the originals, and my unconscious mind will drive up,
packed in an old jalopy. They'll insist
the car is brand new, and try to sell it to me.

I'll play along, check the engine. But I know already
what I'm going to do. I'm going to buy it.
I'm going to drive it all the way to Tierra del Fuego,
and then, at the midnight hour, sell it as scrap.

DIRTY TRICKS CAMPAIGN

Since my fellow men are upwardly mobile
(and luckily the vertical is horizontal),
I hear their orisons, each a turnstile.
The price of admission? Three tin ears.

Me, I don't pray, I'm much too private,
so the congregation exacts some revenge
with a twenty-four-hour automatic pilot
'Love us or leave us we'll track you' binge

of bugs on home, computer and phones.
Calls, coughs and conversations are brief.
If I have my way, they'll become briefer,
but it's not mine, this game no one owns.

What an atmosphere! See the little green men?
And notice the delirium I'm simulating,
the 'heaven and hell nothing's what it seems'
clichés that, yes, interest groups with money

can frame a life with, liberating the canvas.
Petted by the light that has no hand to bite,
they don't turn on themselves — they choose a bystander
(an extra if innocent, star when indicted)

and as they do, data at their disposal,
yoghurt and dates on desert-isle web sites,
or baklava greasing chains of e-mail,
excludes their bios, though not yours and mine.

Anyway, parasites don't kill the host,
and that's good to know: I invited some over,
said, 'Smell fishy, or else play the river,'
eco-improvisations. We, who have croaked

for all these years must face the new music,
admit bodies and souls are bows and arrows,
hand ours to — *deus ex machina!* — Cupid.
There's nothing of us left to shoot. We've grown.

PRISM

I only ask for words to be sung.
Rhythm and melody demote the meaning.
That's as it should be — the many rungs
of any ladder are all underlings.

I just whipped in and out of the prison
in which we hold the women and kids.
We take God's light, pass it through prisms
to get in the mood of our colourful ids.

A personality, too, can be split up.
We pen the men in a fortified loo
where they throw up what they had for breakfast.
Lunch is served from the guards' full moons.

And do I need to mention the wine list?
When our MPs get good and pissed,
we take the Eucharist back to its roots,
flesh flesh again, blood simply blood …

Yes, our music composed in the heavens
effortlessly as moonshine or snow
lifts us out of our creature comforts,
reminds us our bodies are here on loan

for which we pay by harbouring souls
that are never at ease with tracheae,
stateless with no place to call home —
everything they are not is our act,

not that they'd bother to artfully phrase
what I slip into mouths they don't possess.
Should I stop? I'm one of the apes.
We tinker on until we feel blessed,

until we're sure the drifters inside us
are infinite. But can they be trusted?
Lord knows they don't wear their hearts on my sleeve —
I'll lose the shirt, suspend disbelief.

THE MINDERS' BALL

The cagey holy boy following me
is poker-faced when asked his name,
and if one should gob on his being
he's not insulted, calls it rain.

Thus insulated, he grasps the day
like a formula; he knows its end
will confirm suspicious doubts.
The blackboard full, the sun can set.

He says nothing until it has.
They're retroactive, half his claims.
At midnight, taking out the trash
he orders stars to twinkle — games

have bogus rules, and rules in turn
have rules, an infinite succession.
Those of us accustomed to nature
watch it divided into factions:

the chimp, now Ottoman satrap,
endures some Sultan's double vision —
turns out our great ruler is rats!
He'd be a cliché played by a lion.

That's just the thing: 'Surprise, surprise,'
seems to be the guiding spirit.
You like your job? We'll get you fired.
Want to be fired? We'll make you resign.

Love the wife? We'll prove she's a bitch
by bugging, graphing twenty-four hours.
Close-up of the ass if there's an itch.
Up the volume if she clicks at the door.

How did this happen? 'He' became 'we'?
Well, gentlemen, someone's caught out.
No matter: most would call this a dream,
and, if not, witnesses can be bought.

We ourselves have seen it all:
why slip ridiculous sums to strangers?
I solemnly swear that after the ball
we found some god — and finders keepers.

TELEGRAM

Was it you strolling on that funeral pyre?
I thought you said you'd take it lying down.
Like the sun, you move slowly on fire.
If I were either one of you, I'd run.

To hell with decorum! Are we redcoats
to march in step? Baboons are in the bush.
You'll be a passenger soon, the sun your boat,
but how will you reach its full schedule?

I can't play producer; nobody can.
Yet there will have to be a Hollywood stunt
with you, Buster, on a catamaran
beating the horizon to a bloody punch.

Yes, the whole thing will be an illusion:
you travelling to the travelling light.
But its home base is all fission or fusion —
I forget which; a howling bar fight

broke up the professor's lecture on the stars.
The audience swaddled its love of puns
in black-market Taiwanese armour —
when people dress up, they plan to have fun.

Maybe they expected a glamorous subject,
and were bored by the massive energy
of a system without any hyper bipeds.
To seem dignified, we must go to sleep.

Your burning flesh has a constitution,
though its founding fathers are bachelors
whose obsessive subject, these birds about town,
is a speech so free it can be slurred.

I love the fowls, and want them to enjoy
the Indian summer flirting in the shades
we imported for them from the underworld
(it wasn't easy doing business in Hades).

But since we've gone to all this trouble,
the least we can do is breathe the aroma
of a pleasant breeze, square root of rubble —
war is in the air, and here it blows.

VAUDEVILLE

With cracks about White Russian halitosis
Bolsheviks justified camp punishment.
Executives learn to stink by osmosis.
Perhaps Stalin read Marie Antoinette.

The dead use no language, and yet we translate,
Santas with gifts from otherworldly elves
whose lack of personality isn't fake —
at the poles, it's every state of mind for itself.

One night we saw the depths of this silence,
the lengths to which it was willing to go
to cover up all revolutions of the Earth
we needed as alibis for our vertigo.

So we stepped gingerly on the granite
fragments dynamited to build our railroad,
sat the same way in the first-class compartment.
What were our tickets? What our floors

compared to the likelihood one of these days
the dimensions on which we directed behaviour
would take up acting themselves, and their play
kick-box them open like trap doors?

This came to pass, and led to hysteria:
fascists on the right, fascists on the left,
went around peddling a utopia
that turned into a bicycle. Now they take hikes.

It was all an accident: ballads at the core
of our reactions were buried alive.
There are still mornings, so we're consoled —
what is it we love so much about light?

The mimesis stirred up? It's when eyes close clearly
that mere confusion becomes complex.
Chaos, become hell again, if only
to allow gargoyles and ghouls to be etched!

But our commissars snub Lucifer.
The gods had more style, weren't so smug.
Their thunder, exiled by lowing non sequiturs,
was music to our ears, boxed now by thugs.

CALM STORM

It's obvious the powerful do as they please,
and yet afterwards we call these actors
just, miraculous. Everybody freeze.
Are our generals like our political prisoners?

Haven't you heard? In truth, they are.
We've decided to change the rules of drama.
A waste to let a man be only one man;
he should be many, from colonel to slaughtered

conscript, hysterical groom, cut-up bride …
That's more efficient, but there's a problem:
those who can't play themselves, their pride
acts up in the wings — foolish tantrums

would spoil the show. So nobody backstage!
No audience, dialogue or applause.
We've learned from old myths of a golden age —
to be made up, a wheel doesn't need cogs,

can be in the air, house paint, oil …
did I say oil? I meant turpentine.
To clear this mess, let fresh water boil,
not for coffee, as cover for the fires

we didn't set — lightning struck!
Though it's a desert here, no trees,
I slipped one of our sand coolies a buck,
and guess what he brought me? A library.

OPEN SESAME

Some shelter in madness; most rent it out
and live, off the proceeds, a balanced life,
giving and taking, but you are too proud
to line pockets of your house to house fights.

Yet I believe that they can be used,
manipulated even, and why not by us?
Don't sell your soul; just let points of view,
yours and mine, be iron and rust.

I'm here to teach you how to decay.
Custom demands that you slowly descend
from the ancient thresholds of pain
to relationships we can find you out in.

We need you to experience the banality
that's second nature to your fellow men.
Solitude has made you uppity.
We want you to mingle so we can be pals,

and find ourselves experimenting in labs,
heating fugues to an inaudible voice,
whipping one another till we're ready to rat —
confess, I mean — the day we were born.

I've read the manuals: humiliation,
the victim's cicerone, opens up
a forty thieves' cave actually hidden
in Ali Baba's soul — special eye drops

allow the free world to peer into his secrets,
favourite foods and taste in music,
his God fetish, medical diagnosis
that calls epilepsy drug-induced fits.

The pleasure, nay joy, of destroying a man
senile storytellers treat gingerly —
in truth, the torturer is a fan
drilled into the ceiling of morality

which, as we know, is a bare whitewashed room
without the windows for natural air.
Electric light bulbs mean there's no gloom.
If you're beautiful, you won't be scared,

stripped of fig leaves, back in paradise,
each inmate a new Adam or Eve.
As for the ones who come packed in ice,
they're neo-Neanderthals, different species.

How they got here nobody knows,
but nothing inhuman is foreign to us.
We even have museum pieces on loan;
the heads we can't shrink are these marble busts.

TRANCE: A DECLASSIFIED DOCUMENT

I listen to myself, can't believe what I hear,
though if I'm distracted it sounds natural.
If I were asleep, they'd be unreal,
the same phrases I nail down as true.

Repeating over and over, I slowly
dissolve each word, syllable and letter,
except that the liquid tapped is a fetter
locking up for future use what disappears.

Kiss and make up? But whatever for?
Relations should be foreign. Besides, the lips
my own heart poisoned are now deformed.
My dears, I can't help myself — let 'em rip!

I checked with Gallup, and he/she assures me
(by the way, I'm the one called *Dark Prince*)
a jab or two of freedom-fighting helium
can't hurt anybody — nab a balloon, add a pinch

of looking-glass fever, and war is declared
on the air that monopolizes air; this trafficking
of an element in itself means its interest
(either cumulus or rain, that's to be determined)

is in conflict with ours. Ours is more beautiful:
behold it at work on a tree, this woodpecker
looted from a web cartoonist's portfolio —
no old-fashioned Woodrow, our mascot's a predator,

though cute as the old block he's a chip off.
Habits die hard; we take life easily.
Our mentors had trench coats and Kalashnikovs.
Our bombs are dropped by the birds and the bees

we repay weekly with a real love of nature,
though we ask science to keep it in line.
To the naked eye, our venom is slime,
but under microscopes some petals flower

into objects supernatural. That rings a bell
I knelt near the other day, vowing to take
its digital photo to celebrate my awakening
from classified worlds into our leaky hell,

if you'll pardon the mild-mannered theology.
The only demons I display are gentrified,
clear their shaved throats, and leave no debris,
four fragrant horsemen in my four-wheel drive.

A DISPOSITION OF THE ANTIQUITIES

You know how it is with dictators and flunkies ...
get as many citizens as possible involved
in the jack-of-all-trades firing squads,
Jills too, divers ages, creeds, ethnicities ...

That way, with guilt, it's share and share alike.
But why serve up so jam-packed an idea?
We need something we can empty, an ear:
when chips are down, it's easiest to bribe

with babble about it being a roulette wheel.
Words are a ball in no-man's land,
especially mispronounced by shifting sands,
museums trashed, bronze poses effete,

withdrawn from a 5,000-year-old account,
the Mesopotamian. A new world forwards
open-hearted tips of the hat to feudal
and space-age under-the-table body counts

whose survivors we ask how all went, looking away
to focus on nothing in particular, the distance
resettled by the usual heroines and princes,
a landscape to some, to others eternity

but to this boy more of our enemy's gold.
Yes, we occupy what we meditate on,
frame, without painting, a scene with our brawn
lest something escape us. Our own scent grows cold,

but luckily we didn't come east to search souls,
ours or the locals'. That would be intrusive.
We're here to liberate and barter for the looters'
antiquities — resell them as 'postmodern dolls',

or some other code name we'll come up with
for the black markets that could be called white,
any colour in fact. Why put up a fight
when the opponent is our own rich vocabulary?

ACKNOWLEDGEMENTS

Several of the poems in *Bastardi Puri* have appeared — sometimes in different forms and under different titles — in *ALIF, Jusoor, Maisonneuve, Books in Canada* and *zingmagazine*.

The author is grateful to the Canada Council, the Ontario Arts Council and the Toronto Arts Council for their support.

Walid Bitar was born in Beirut in 1961. He immigrated to Canada in 1969. He has taught English, most recently at Lebanese American University. His previous poetry collections are *Maps with Moving Parts* (Brick, 1988) and 2 *Guys on Holy Land* (Wesleyan University Press/University Press of New England, 1993).